FLOWER•FAIRIES
BIRTHDAY•BOOK

FLOWER・FAIRIES BIRTHDAY・BOOK

with illustrations by
Cicely Mary Barker

FREDERICK WARNE

FREDERICK WARNE

Published by the Penguin Group
27 Wrights Lane, London W8 5TZ, England
Penguin Books USA Inc., 375 Hudson Street, New York, N.Y. 10014, USA
Penguin Books Australia Ltd, Ringwood, Victoria, Australia
Penguin Books Canada Ltd, 10 Alcorn Avenue, Toronto, Ontario,
Canada M4V 3B2
Penguin Books (NZ) Ltd, 182-190 Wairau Road, Auckland 10, New Zealand

Penguin Books Ltd, Registered Offices: Harmondsworth, Middlesex, England

First published in 1989
This edition with new reproductions, published 1992

5 7 9 10 8 6 4

ISBN 0 7232 3785 9

Printed and bound in Great Britain by
William Clowes Limited, Beccles and London

The Pine Tree Fairy

JANUARY

January 1

....
....
....
....

January 2

....
....
....

January 3

....
....
....
....

January 4

....

....

....

January 5

....

....

....

January 6

....

....

....

January 7

....

....

....

January 8

....

....

....

January 9

....

....

....

January 10

....

....

....

January 11

....

....

....

January 12

....
....
....

January 13

....
....
....

January 14

....
....
....

January 15

....
....
....

The Snowdrop Fairy

January 16

January 17

January 18

January 19

January 20

....

....

....

....

January 21

....

....

....

....

The Winter Aconite Fairy

January 22

....
....
....
....

January 23

....
....
....

January 24

....
....
....

January 25

....
....
....
....

January 26

....

....

....

January 27

....

....

....

January 28

....

....

....

January 29

....

....

....

January 30

....
....
....
....

January 31

....
....
....
....

The Yew Fairy

FEBRUARY

February 1

....
....
....
....

February 2

....
....
....

February 3

....
....
....
....

February 4

....

....

....

February 5

....

....

....

February 6

....

....

....

February 7

....

....

....

February 8

....
....
....
....

February 9

....
....
....

February 10

February 11

February 12

February 13

The Rush-Grass and
Cotton-Grass Fairies

February 14

....
....
....
....

February 15

....
....
....
....

February 16

....
....
....
....

February 17

....
....
....

February 18

....
....
....

February 19

....
....
....

The Crocus Fairies

February 20

....

....

....

....

February 21

....

....

....

....

February 22

....

....

....

....

February 23

....

....

....

....

February 24

....

....

....

February 25

....

....

....

February 26

....

....

....

February 27

....

....

....

February 28

....

....

....

....

February 29

....

....

....

....

The Blackthorn Fairy

MARCH

March 1

....

....

....

March 2

....

....

....

March 3

....

....

....

March 4

March 5

March 6

March 7

March 8

....

....

....

March 9

My Birthday ....

....

....

March 10

....

....

....

....

March 11

....

....

....

March 12

....

....

....

March 13

....

....

....

The Daffodil Fairy

March 14

....

....

....

March 15

....

....

....

March 16

....

....

....

March 17

....

....

....

March 18

....
....
....
....

March 19

....
....
....

March 20

....
....
....

March 21

....
....
....

The Almond Blossom Fairy

March 22

....
....
....
....

March 23

....
....
....
....

March 24

....
....
....
....

March 25

....
....
....
....

March 26

....

....

....

March 27

....

....

....

March 28

....

....

....

March 29

....

....

....

March 30

....

....

....

March 31

....

....

....

The Narcissus Fairy

APRIL

April 1

....
....
....
....

April 2

....
....
....
....

April 3

....
....
....
....

April 4

....

....

....

April 5

....

....

....

April 6

....

....

....

April 7

....

....

....

April 8

....
....
....
....

April 9

....
....
....
....

April 10

....

....

....

....

April 11

....

....

....

....

April 12

....

....

....

....

April 13

....

....

....

....

The Wild Cherry Blossom Fairy

April 14

....

....

....

....

April 15

....

....

....

....

April 16

....

....

....

....

April 17

....

....

....

....

April 18

....

....

....

....

April 19

....

....

....

....

The Laburnum Fairy

April 20

....
....
....
....

April 21

....
....
....
....

April 22

....
....
....
....

April 23

....
....
....
....

April 24

....

....

....

....

April 25

....

....

....

....

April 26

....

....

....

....

April 27

....

....

....

....

April 28

....
....
....
....

April 29

....
....
....
....

April 30

....
....
....
....

The Tulip Fairy

MAY

May 1

....
....
....
....

May 2

....
....
....
....

May 3

....
....
....
....

May 4

....

....

....

May 5

....

....

....

May 6

....

....

....

May 7

....

....

....

May 8

....
....
....
....

May 9

....
....
....
....

May 10

May 11

May 12

May 13

The Beech Tree Fairy

May 14

....

....

....

May 15

....

....

....

May 16

....

....

....

May 17

....

....

....

May 18

....
....
....

May 19

....
....
....

May 20

....
....
....

The Lilac Fairy

May 21

....
....
....
....

May 22

....
....
....

May 23

....
....
....

May 24

....
....
....

May 25

....

....

....

....

May 26

....

....

....

....

May 27

....

....

....

....

May 28

....

....

....

....

May 29

....

....

....

May 30

....

....

....

May 31

....

....

....

The Buttercup Fairy

JUNE

June 1

....

....

....

June 2

....

....

....

June 3

....

....

....

June 4

....

....

....

....

June 5

....

....

....

June 6

....

....

....

June 7

....

....

....

June 8

....
....
....
....

June 9

....
....
....
....

June 10

....

....

....

June 11

....

....

....

June 12

....

....

....

June 13

....

....

....

The Willow Fairy

June 14

....

....

....

June 15

....

....

....

June 16

....

....

....

June 17

June 18

June 19

June 20

Mums birthday

The White Bindweed Fairy

June 21

....
....
....
....

June 22

....
....
....
....

June 23

....
....
....
....

June 24

....
....
....
....

June 25

....
....
....

June 26

....
....
....

June 27

....
....
....

June 28

....
....
....

June 29

....

....

....

....

June 30

....

....

....

The Rose Fairy

JULY

July 1

....
....
....
....

July 2

....
....
....
....

July 3

....
....
....
....

July 4

....

....

....

....

July 5

....

....

....

....

July 6

....

....

....

....

July 7

....

....

....

....

July 8

....
....
....
....

July 9

....
....
....
....

July 10

....

....

....

....

July 11

....

....

....

....

July 12

....

....

....

....

July 13

....

....

....

....

The Pink Fairies

July 14

July 15

July 16

July 17

July 18

July 19

Chris's birthday

The Lavender Fairy

July 20

....
....
....
....

July 21

....
....
....

July 22

....
....
....
....

July 23

....
....
....

July 24

....
....
....
....

July 25

....
....
....
....

July 26

....
....
....
....

July 27

....
....
....
....

July 28

July 29

Oly's Birthday! ♡

July 30

July 31

The Sweet Pea Fairies

AUGUST

August 1

....
....
....
....

August 2

....
....
....
....

August 3

....
....
....
....

August 4

....

....

....

August 5

....

....

....

August 6

....

....

....

August 7

....

....

....

August 8

August 9

August 10

....
....
....

August 11

....
....
....

August 12

....
....
....

August 13

....
....
....

The Horned Poppy Fairy

August 14

....
....
....

August 15

....
....
....

August 16

....
....
....

August 17

August 18

August 19

August 20

The Heliotrope Fairy

August 21

....

....

....

August 22

....

....

....

August 23

....

....

....

August 24

....

....

....

August 25

....
....
....
....

August 26

....
....
....
....

August 27

....
....
....

August 28

....
....
....

August 29

....

....

....

....

August 30

....

....

....

August 31

....

....

....

....

The Rose Hip Fairy

SEPTEMBER

September 1

....
....
....
....

September 2

....
....
....
....

September 3

....
....
....

September 4

....

....

....

September 5

....

....

....

September 6

....

....

....

September 7

....

....

....

September 8

September 9

September 10

....

....

....

....

September 11

....

....

....

....

September 12

....

....

....

....

September 13

....

....

....

....

The Blackberry Fairy

September 14

....

....

....

September 15

....

....

....

September 16

....

....

....

September 17

....

....

....

September 18

September 19

September 20

The Michaelmas Daisy Fairy

September 21

Claires birthday

September 22

September 23

September 24

September 25

....

....

....

September 26

....

....

....

September 27

....

....

....

September 28

....

....

....

September 29

September 30

The Elderberry Fairy

OCTOBER

October 1

....
....
....
....

October 2

....
....
....
....

October 3

....
....
....
....

October 4

....
....
....
....

October 5

....
....
....
....

October 6

....
....
....
....

October 7

....
....
....
....

October 8

....
....
....
....

October 9

....
....
....
....

October 10

....

....

....

October 11

....

....

....

October 12

....

....

....

October 13

....

....

....

The Beechnut Fairy

October 14

....
....
....
....

October 15

....
....
....
....

October 16

....
....
....
....

October 17

....
....
....
....

October 18

....
....
....
....

October 19

....
....
....
....

October 20

....
....
....
....

The Sloe Fairy

October 21

....
....
....
....

October 22

....
....
....
....

October 23

....
....
....
....

October 24

....
....
....
....

October 25

....

....

....

October 26

....

....

....

October 27

....

....

....

October 28

....

....

....

October 29

....

....

....

October 30

....

....

....

October 31

....

....

....

The Sweet Chestnut Fairy

NOVEMBER

November 1

....
....
....
....

November 2

....
....
....

November 3

....
....
....

November 4

....

....

....

November 5

....

....

....

November 6

....

....

....

November 7

....

....

....

November 8

....

....

....

....

November 9

....

....

....

....

November 10

....
....
....
....

November 11

....
....
....
....

November 12

....
....
....
....

November 13

....
....
....
....

The Old-Man's-Beard Fairy

November 14

....

....

....

November 15

....

....

....

November 16

....

....

....

November 17

....

....

....

November 18

November 19

*Begging for apples on St Clement's
Day—23rd November*

The Winter Jasmine Fairy

November 20

....
....
....
....

November 21

....
....
....
....

November 22

....
....
....
....

November 23

....
....
....
....

November 24

....

....

....

November 25

....

....

....

November 26

....

....

....

November 27

....

....

....

November 28

....

....

....

November 29

....

....

....

November 30

....

....

....

The Lords-and-Ladies Fairy

DECEMBER

December 1

....
....
....
....

December 2

....
....
....
....

December 3

....
....
....
....

December 4

....
....
....
....

December 5

....
....
....
....

December 6

....
....
....
....

December 7

....
....
....
....

December 8

December 9

December 10

December 11

....

....

....

December 12

....

....

....

December 13

....

....

....

December 14

....

....

....

The Holly Fairy

December 15

···
···
···

December 16

···
···
···

December 17

···
···
···

December 18

December 19

December 20

December 21

The Christmas Tree Fairy

December 22

....
....
....
....

December 23

....
....
....
....

December 24

....
....
....

December 25

....
....
....
....

December 26

....

....

....

December 27

....

....

....

December 28

....

....

....

December 29

....

....

....

December 30

....

....

....

December 31

....

....

....

SOURCES OF ILLUSTRATIONS

July
The Rose Fairy   *Flower Fairies of the Summer*
The Pink Fairies   *Flower Fairies of the Garden*
The Lavender Fairy   *Flower Fairies of the Garden*

August
The Sweet Pea Fairies   *Flower Fairies of the Garden*
The Horned Poppy Fairy   *Flower Fairies of the Wayside*
The Heliotrope Fairy   *Flower Fairies of the Garden*

September
The Rose Hip Fairy   *Flower Fairies of the Autumn*
The Blackberry Fairy   *Flower Fairies of the Autumn*
The Michaelmas Daisy Fairy   *Flower Fairies of the Autumn*

October
The Elderberry Fairy   *Flower Fairies of the Autumn*
The Beechnut Fairy   *Flower Fairies of the Autumn*
The Sloe Fairy   *Flower Fairies of the Autumn*

November
The Sweet Chestnut Fairy   *Flower Fairies of the Trees*
The Old-Man's-Beard Fairy   *Flower Fairies of the Winter*
The Winter Jasmine Fairy   *Flower Fairies of the Winter*

December
The Lords and Ladies Fairy   *Flower Fairies of the Winter*
The Holly Fairy   *Flower Fairies of the Winter*
The Christmas Tree Fairy   *Flower Fairies of the Winter*